First Then, First Now

By the mid-1900s, speculation as to the vast potential for naturally occurring compounds in pest management and crop production systems was beginning to gain momentum. Building on the most promising applications for a small group of natural products, Valent BioSciences Corporation (VBC) pioneered the biopesticide industry over 40 years ago by introducing the world to *Bacillus thuringiensis* (Bt) and Plant Growth Regulator (PGR) technologies. Operating then as the Agricultural Division of Abbott Laboratories, VBC continues today as the world's largest researcher, developer, and marketer of biorational products.

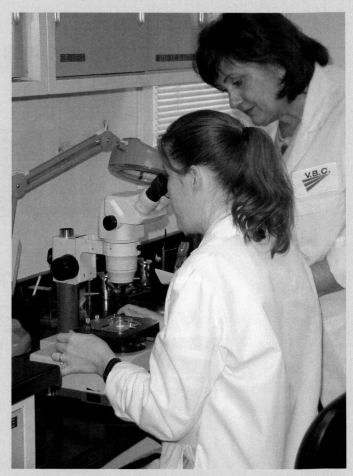

The wide range of agronomic factors governing crop production, coupled with the unique attributes of biorationals, provides VBC with endless opportunites to deliver value. Unrivaled experience in the biorational sphere has helped identify a long list of crop/product/program benefits that translate to the bottom-line.

VBC's corporate vision is unique: to be the worldwide leader in the commercialization and supply of low risk, environmentally compatible agricultural and forestry products. These products enhance crop productivity and add value for the grower.

Why Did We Produce This Guide?

Welcome to the **Guide to Understanding and Evaluating Biorational Products**, from Valent BioSciences Corporation (VBC). As the title suggests, this guide is intended to provide participants in the food and fiber production chain with fundamental information on biorational products and their role in cropping systems and sound business strategy. For the purposes of this book, the term "biorational" refers to the microbial and plant growth regulator (PGR) categories of agricultural products.

This guide was developed to support the growing realization that biorational products have the potential to contribute substantially to bottom-line profit. Also contributing to increasing global interest in these products is a growing emphasis on organics and integrated pest management (IPM), integrated fruit production (IFP) systems, as well as fundamental issues such as resistance and residue management.

This book is intended for broad use by growers and farm managers, agronomists and consultants, extension specialists, researchers and educators, and by input suppliers who field questions surrounding these products. It does not provide application rates and timing information for use with biorational products, but rather explains how these products are used, for whom they are best suited, and examines the basic value proposition of biorationals.

How are biorational products important for the grower, advisor, or ag supply distributor? What unique attributes do these products possess that make them a logical fit in today's market? These are important questions that demand answers.

continued >

Why Did We Produce This Guide? (continued)

Performance and profitability are the starting points for biorational use. This guide focuses on products and product categories with a proven track record, and operates from the premise that efficacy, consistency, and performance are a given. It also provides information on how to evaluate these products, and to differentiate high quality biorationals from products that cannot meet these basic requirements.

Simply put, the most important attribute of biorational products is that they add value. In many ways, the value proposition is much different than traditional ag chemicals. In this book, we will examine in detail how this value is delivered not only to growers, but to each link in the food value chain.

As the market leader in biorational products for more than 40 years, no other company is better equipped to provide this information than Valent BioSciences. As the world's largest producer of biorational products, VBC has a responsibility to ensure that these products are accurately represented and clearly understood by all who might benefit from their unique qualities. We hope that you profit from this publication, and welcome any feedback you might have.

Valent BioSciences Corporation

TABLE OF CONTENTS

VALENT BIOSCIENCES
CORPORATION

BIORATIONALS OVERVIEW

What does "Biorational" Mean?

Biorational (bī ō ′rash ən-'l)

1 An active ingredient or formulation that is effective controlling pests and is typically derived from biological or natural origins.

2 Characterized as providing added value to the end user, being highly targeted and efficacious while having low impact on both the environment and non-target living organisms.

VALENT BIOSCIENCES
CORPORATION

Types of Biorationals

Biorational products include microbial products with unique pest management properties, such as certain kinds of bacteria, viruses, fungi, and nematodes. It also includes biochemical products that have dramatic effects on plant and insect growth and development. These products include plant growth regulators (PGRs), hormones, enzymes, plant extracts, and pheromones.

Because of their unique properties, biorational products offer a range of benefits, many of which cannot be obtained through programs that are limited to traditional chemicals.

Most importantly, biorational products add value by improving crop quality and packout. Return on investment (ROI) to the grower then translates into added value for other links in the production and distribution chain.

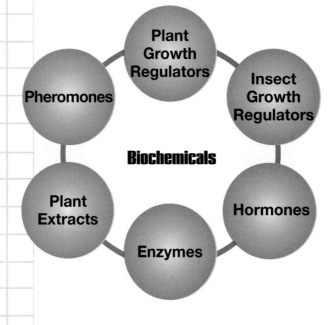

The Agricultural System

Production agriculture is a highly complex system where growers and farm managers control inputs and processes in an effort to maximize quality, efficiency, and economic results.

As an input category, crop protection and crop enhancement chemicals help define the success of a given system. As such, biorational products have tremendous potential to significantly impact bottom-line performance by helping growers meet these fundamental objectives.

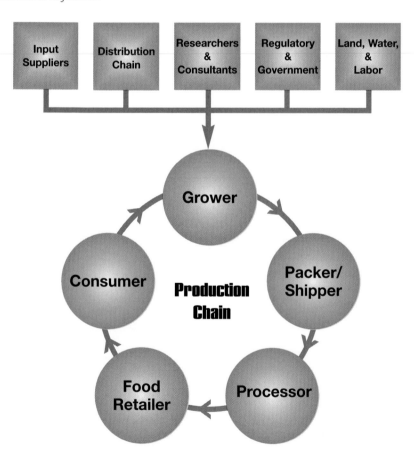

| Input Suppliers | Distribution Chain | Researchers & Consultants | Regulatory & Government | Land, Water, & Labor |

Production Chain

Grower → Packer/Shipper → Processor → Food Retailer → Consumer → Grower

Value in the agricultural production chain begins with the grower. The grower's ability to produce a high quality crop makes for a profitable business, as that value is delivered down the chain to the packer shipper, the processor, the retailer, and ultimately the consumer. Closing the system, consumer preferences and buying decisions help guide what the grower does.

Understanding Biorational Products

VALENT BioSciences CORPORATION

The Global Trend

Biorational product usage includes PGRs, bioinsecticides, bioherbicides, and biofungicides. Over the past several years, use of biorationals has increased dramatically in each of those categories. (see tables). With respect to agricultural applications, several factors have combined to account for this increase. These factors include:

■ The loss of older chemistries in many markets

The Food Quality Protection Act of 1999 resulted in the cancellation of many traditional chemistries, particularly in the organophosphate and carbamate classes.

■ Increased emphasis on resistance management programs

As the number of pesticide choices have been reduced, growers are more apt to protect the life span of the products that remain. Also, many of the newer chemistries are particularly susceptible to resistance.

Biorational Market Growth Rate		
Time Period	Crop Protection Market % Annual Growth Rate In Real Terms	Biorational Market % Annual Growth Rate In Real Terms
1970-1979	6.8	0.1
1980-1989	2.2	8.0
1990-1999	0.1	9.0
2000-2004	-2.3	10.0
Forecasted After 2005	0.75*	6.0**

*Market growth limited by market saturation, generics, and regulatory impact

**Market growth slower due to the lack of introduction of new products.

Sources: Phillips McDougall; Agrow Report 2004: Biopesticide, Biocontrol, and Semio-Chemical Markets; Scientific Consultants 2002: Biopesticides — 6th Edition; Volume 1 — Markets; Volume 4 — Companies

Toward Biorationals

▉ Increased commitment to integrated pest management programs (IPM) by key influencers

Key influencers are typically classified as extension specialists, agronomists, and consultants who advise growers. In most countries, these influencers bear the responsibility of shepherding increased IPM implementation, driven by public policy and buyer requirements.

▉ Advances in formulation technology

Advances in formulation technology have made biopesticides easier to use.

▉ Increased understanding of the effects of PGRs

In many crops, the competitive landscape has made PGRs an indispensable part of the growing program. Also, advances in the science behind plant growth regulators has resulted in new products with more widespread application.

▉ Growing consumer awareness about pesticide use

As science and information technology have advanced, so has consumer awareness regarding pesticide residues on food. This awareness has helped shape public policy, which in turn has resulted in increased use of biorationals.

▉ Increased demand for organically grown food

While biorational products are a critical component of traditional agricultural programs, crop protection programs in organic production are largely dependent on biorationals. Organic acreage has increased by nearly 400% in the past 10 years.

▉ Increase in organic and IPM-related branding

With increased demand has come increased branding opportunities. Food retailers and marketing associations have realized market advantages related to crop production practices that embrace biorationals.

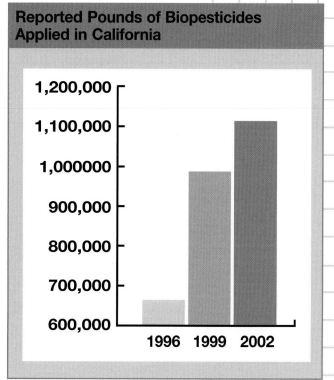

Reported Pounds of Biopesticides Applied in California

Source: California Department of Pesticide Regulation

Understanding Biorational Products

VALENT BIOSCIENCES CORPORATION

Sound Business Sense

Q: When Does Using a Biorational Product Make Sense?

A: Any time a grower wants to maximize profits using sustainable crop production programs.

In this Guide, we examine a wide range of benefits that can translate into bottom-line improvement for a variety of crops, and how those benefits are delivered through use of biorational products. This pragmatic, profit-driven approach will help both growers and advisors make informed decisions about the potential for biorationals in their operations.

Identifying Your Objectives

Different growers have different priorities, but all center around maintaining a profitable enterprise while bringing the consumer a high quality product. Check off those factors with the potential to positively impact your bottom line:

☐ Crop quality and productivity

☐ Pest resistance management activities

☐ Maximizing benefits from precise application timing

☐ Harvest management advantages

☐ Regulatory and worker safety advantages

☐ Marketing advantages

VBC specializes in products that deliver on each count!

VALENT BIOSCIENCES CORPORATION

Misconceptions about Biorational Products

Because biorationals are nontraditional pesticides, there remains a certain amount of confusion regarding their nature, their use, and their benefits. A lack of understanding about biorationals often helps perpetuate misconceptions about these products. Dispelling misconceptions about biorational products is one of the primary aims of this guide.

Most misconceptions about biorationals draw from the broad nature of the category itself. All too often, "natural" products enter the market place with claims that cannot be substantiated. These products are overpromoted and, in some instances, may perform poorly. This muddies the water for prospective users of quality products and those who might recommend them. Sound science and verifiable performance history are the keys to telling the difference.

The following is a list of common misconceptions surrounding the biorational category:

■ Biorational products don't work.

■ Biorational products are expensive.

■ Biorationals are complicated and difficult to use.

■ Biorationals are intended to replace traditional chemicals.

■ Biorationals are only for use in organic growing systems, and are not used in mainstream agriculture.

■ All biorational products are created equal.

■ Biorational products are not reliable.

On the following pages, we'll explore the truth behind each of these misconceptions.

VALENT BioSciences.
CORPORATION

7 Misconceptions about Biorational Products

MISCONCEPTION #1

Biorational products don't work.

The Reality: Tens of thousands of growers worldwide use biorational products regularly, products that perform consistently and at a very high level. In many markets, these products are not only beneficial, but a necessary part of a grower's program.

Still, there are some products marketed as biorational that either do not meet the claims of the manufacturer, or can not perform consistently. Unfortunately, these products contaminate the biorational category. One of the primary reasons for this guide is to give people the ability to differentiate between products that work and products that do not.

Most biorationals are characterized as having a biological or "natural" origin. That means that any product made up of "natural" elements can be lumped in with biorationals. The market is crowded with products that contain a mixture of natural components that have dubious worth. In other words, while highly efficacious biorational products exist, that doesn't mean that every natural product will deliver value.

The good news is that high quality biorational products with a proven history of efficacy and consistency are becoming more and more important among top growers and farm managers. In addition to their pesticidal and plant growth properties, these products possess valuable attributes and features that meet unique grower needs.

MISCONCEPTION #2

Biorational products are expensive.

The Reality: This misconception surrounds both microbial products and PGRs, but for two different reasons.

Microbial products compare favorably on price with most traditional insecticides, but they can also reduce the total program cost when used along side the more expensive newer chemistries currently available *Bacillus thuringiensis* (Bt) is also perfect for late-season sprays when preharvest restrictions for traditional products can negatively impact market window opportunities.

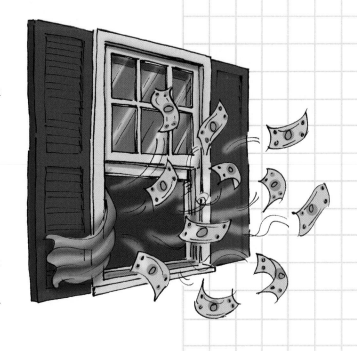

PGRs, on the other hand, are an investment that increases crop value by influencing key plant or fruit characteristics during the crop cycle. The cost of these products is a fraction of the anticipated return. In its simplest form, it's a matter of increasing inputs to increase outputs. As one table grape grower from California so eloquently put it, "Any time you can spend an extra dollar to make an extra five, you do it."

VALENT BIOSCIENCES.
CORPORATION

MISCONCEPTION #3

Biorationals are complicated and difficult to use.

The Reality: Most modern farmers easily qualify to use biorationals. A large percentage of top growers already use them, as millions of acres of cropland receive biorational product applications each year.

Are rates and application timing important with biorationals? Absolutely. Do scouting activities maximize the benefits gained through many biorational products? Without a doubt. Is plant health and crop condition an important factor in how effective these products will be? Most definitely. But most growers are already managing these same variables, even in traditional programs.

The truth is that growers who aren't using biorationals typically lack exposure to these products, not the skills to use them. As with any chemical, biorational or otherwise, novice users depend more heavily on product support at first, less so as they gain experience. Therefore it is especially important for new users to choose a supplier with a strong support network in place.

MISCONCEPTION #4

Biorationals are intended to replace traditional chemicals.

The Reality: Biorationals are not replacements for traditional chemicals, but are simply another important instrument in the grower's toolbox. In the case of microbial insecticides and nematicides, biorationals control pests just as traditional products do, but also provide additional benefits such as resistance management, residue management, and environmental and human health benefits.

The key is that biorational products provide a valuable piece to the puzzle. Just as using a single traditional product to control all pests wouldn't make sense, biorational products are best used as one element of a comprehensive program that accounts for all of the variables growers are able to manipulate.

In fact, some might argue that the best time to use microbial products is when a new chemical product comes to the market place. Combining the two into a sustainable program creates value both economically and environmentally.

MISCONCEPTION #5

Biorationals are only for use in organic growing systems, and are not used in mainstream agriculture.

The Reality: It is true that one of the benefits of most biorational products is that they are approved for use in organic growing systems. It is not true that these products are intended solely for use on organically grown crops. Only a small percentage of the total amount of biorationals consumed each year are applied to acreage under organic production.

In some regions of the world, nearly 100% of crops such as tomatoes, peppers, lettuce, grapes, or rice receive at least one biorational application per season. Market penetration for biorational products is actually highest among large-scale growers.

Still, the same benefits exist for small and medium-sized growers — conventional or organic. They are used by entrepreneurial growers with a business approach to growing crops, people who understand the difference between an investment and an expenditure. Biorationals are used by people who support their decision making process with technical evidence and financial soundness. These growing operations can be either organic growers or traditional agriculture growers.

MISCONCEPTION #6

All biorational products are created equal.

The Reality: Many people reason that because biorationals are derived from biological or natural origins, all biorational products are the same. In reality, the opposite is true. All biorational products have attributes specifically linked to unique traits in subspecies or strains. How well these traits are expressed is closely tied to the manufacturing process itself.

The highly complex make up of biorationals demands the utmost skill and precision for manufacturing. The guiding principles for use of biological insecticides and PGRs may be the same, but it's important to understand that each biorational product is as unique as the company and quality control system that produces it. While competing products may arise from the same microbial species, for example, the strains that produce the pesticidal toxins or PGRs are unique to every manufacturer.

MISCONCEPTION #7

Biorational products are not reliable.

The Reality: Many biorational products are reliable, but some are not. Being able to tell the difference is the key to performance meeting expectation.

Still, there is a list of variables that contributes to how well even the best products perform, including the formulation technology, proper use and timing, rates, spray coverage, weather, and plant health (nutrition, presence of diseases, etc.).

Ironically, these same factors impact how well a traditional chemical performs. But the wide gap that exists between quality biorationals and suspect biorational products means that when the desired effects are not achieved, growers are much more likely to question the product than the practice.

All the more reason to choose only biorational products with an established history of quality and consistency. Research shows that when applied correctly, VBC biorationals perform as consistently as any of their traditional counterparts.

Understanding Biorational Benefits

Biorational products have demonstrable value for each link in the production chain, but that value begins with benefits derived by the grower. Input value at the grower level is usually measured by return on investment (ROI), where biorationals have a positive impact through a variety of benefits.

ROI Benefits Associated with Biorational Products:

■ Enhanced Crop Quality and Shelf Life

■ Resistance Management

■ Maintaining Beneficial Populations

■ Residue Management

■ Labor and Harvest Flexibility

■ Differentiating the Offering

■ Worker Safety

■ Environmental Safety

How these benefits are prioritized varies by application and operation, but the key to evaluating biorationals is in drawing the connection between expenditure and anticipated return.

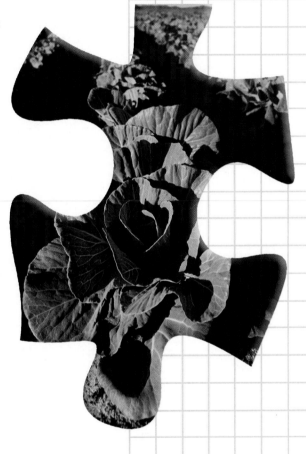

VALENT BIOSCIENCES CORPORATION

Benefits in Crop Quality

The term *crop quality* encompasses a wide range of crop attributes that result in a better bottom-line for the grower. These attributes can refer to a higher grade crop, better yield, or physical characteristics that enhance the crop's value. Growers are quick to incorporate inputs that significantly improve the quality of their crop, as quality goes right to the bottom-line.

While specific benefits vary by application, use of biorationals can result in a variety of effects that impact crop quality. These include:

☑ **Fruit size:** Perhaps the most widely recognized benefit of PGRs. Higher grade fruit equals a better price at the farmgate.

☑ **Packout:** Larger fruits means more volume per hectare.

☑ **Shape and color:** Critical variables that affect the saleability of many crops, and can be optimized through use of biorationals.

☑ **Absence of defects:** Use of biorationals in a pest control program often leads to better control and better quality fruit. The ability to apply biorationals close to harvest also protects against late season insect pressure.

☑ **Firmness and shelf life:** Fruit firmness directly impacts shelf and transit life, which may also open doors to profitable new markets.

☑ **Taste and texture:** Both are variables directly related to the physiological attributes of the fruit.

☑ **Plant health:** Directly related to crop quality. Some biorationals boost plant defenses or have the potential to increase root mass.

☑ **Absence of toxic residues:** A critical factor in fresh produce and processed food markets, *i.e.* baby food.

In most cases, use of biorational products brings about a combination of these benefits, and delivers quality from the grower all the way to the consumer.

Benefits in Resistance Management

Insect, weed, and disease populations can develop resistance to pesticides quickly. Growers employ a variety of tactics – including chemical rotation – to prevent or delay this from happening. With a limited number of pest control products available, the loss of a single important product can be devastating.

Resistance management strategies focus on protecting the lifespan of the pest control products in the grower's toolbox. Because of their unique modes of action, microbial insecticides and fungicides have long been cornerstones of pesticide resistance management programs around the world.

Microbial products have much more complex modes of action than their traditional counterparts, which means it is somewhat more difficult for insects and plant pathogens to develop resistance to these products. In fact, cases of observed resistance to microbial products are relatively limited, especially when used in an IPM program. A related benefit is that microbial products can be used in rotation with each other to maintain an all biological program without fear of resistance.

VALENT BIOSCIENCES
CORPORATION

Benefits in Residue Management

Increasing consumer awareness toward the nature and application of pesticides is one of the driving forces behind the growing biorational trend. The global regulatory community supports consumer demand through rule making authorities that manage pesticide residues on food. Residue management refers to the grower's need to deliver produce that is residue free or within acceptable levels.

A key benefit of biorational products is their ability to help the grower deliver produce with the absence of pesticide residue, or residue levels within regulatory parameters. This benefit is especially important late in the season, when growers need a pesticide application to protect a crop that's nearing harvest.

A related benefit is in critical export markets, where a single failed inspection can mean the end of a buyer/seller relationship. Similarly in domestic markets, advances in recordkeeping and traceback capabilities have linked the produce buyer directly to the field from which the produce originates. A breach of acceptable residue levels linked to a farm operation can be devastating.

Benefits through Flexibility and Harvest Management

In some ways, flexibility benefits derived from biorationals overlap with residue management benefits. But in addition to microbial pesticides providing the grower with more late-season application options, plant growth regulators allow growers to manipulate harvest time and the length of the harvest season.

From a purely economic standpoint, market prices are linked to supply and demand. The difference of a few weeks in bringing a product to market can mean a dramatic difference in price. In many markets, PGRs are used to significantly delay harvest in order to take advantage of market windows when supply wanes and prices rise. This effect is also closely linked to fruit size with many crops, inasmuch as fruit that stays on the plant longer continues to develop.

Harvest management is also closely linked to labor considerations, a major issue for growers dependent on a large labor force for harvesting. The ability to extend the harvest season in a large grove or orchard — while keeping all the harvested fruit at optimum maturity — gives growers considerable flexibility with regard to time, labor, and ultimately, expense.

VALENT BIOSCIENCES CORPORATION

Benefits through Environmental Safety

One cannot overstate the importance of a grower being a good steward of the land. More and more, environmental stewardship and Best Management Practices are at the forefront of commercial farming operations. Indeed, the art of being a top-notch grower is maximizing ROI while at the same time being a responsible steward. Biorational products deliver on both fronts by providing solutions with a low impact to the environment without sacrificing effectiveness.

VBC's biorationals have minimal toxicity to birds, fish, or bees, help to maintain beneficial insect populations, and break down quickly. Just as with many of the other benefits described here, biorationals work best while providing these in a program alongside traditional chemicals.

Biorational User Profile: The Grower

A grower that uses biorational products typically exhibits some or all of these traits:

☑ Bottom-line focused

☑ Entrepreneurial

☑ Needs inputs that enhance crop quality

☑ Interested in technology

☑ Uses various means to manage resistance

☑ Grows produce for export or fresh market, or sells to demanding food processors

☑ Has numerous long-term customers

☑ Relies on expert labor management strategies

☑ Employs Best Management Practices

☑ Times crop to meet premium market window

All VBC product development begins with grower needs.

VALENT BIOSCIENCES CORPORATION

Biorational User Profile: The Technical Advisor

Technical advisors include academia, research and extension specialists, consultants, and crop advisors. An advisor who typically recommends biorational products exhibits some or all of these traits:

☑ Well versed in pesticide technology

☑ Emphasizes resistance management strategies

☑ Has training in agricultural economics

☑ Emphasizes productivity

☑ Emphasizes justifying recommendations through research

☑ In tune with changing consumer preferences

☑ Seeks to provide leadership in area of IPM

☑ Understands what makes a quality biorational product

VBC products help advisors meet these objectives with confidence.

Biorational User Profile: The Distribution Chain

Members of the distribution chain range from regional and in-field sales people to the person behind the counter at a local dealership. A dealer/distributor who typically recommends biorational products exhibits some or all of these traits:

- ☑ Seeks continuous education on pesticide technology
- ☑ Serves all segments — has a broad customer base
- ☑ Has customers who are technologically inclined
- ☑ Has customers who want to reach export markets
- ☑ Wants a broad portfolio of complementary products
- ☑ Helps customers to manage life-span of traditional chemicals
- ☑ Needs products that perform consistently
- ☑ Needs products that store well
- ☑ Needs a dependable supply chain
- ☑ Appreciates quality technical support

A dealer's reputation is on the line with every sale. VBC provides the support that helps dealers deliver service to their customers.

VALENT BIOSCIENCES CORPORATION

Biorational User Profile: The Consumer & Policy Maker

A consumer or policy maker who typically embraces biorational products exhibits some or all of these traits:

☑ Wants produce that is residue free

☑ Wants produce that is free of defects

☑ Wants produce that is of a premium grade

☑ Wants a consistent supply of quality produce

☑ Willing to pay a premium for produce grown under IPM

☑ Wants growers to be good stewards of the land

VBC helps growers deliver tangible benefits to the end user.

Understanding Microbials

VALENT BIOSCIENCES
CORPORATION

Understanding Microbial Products

Microbial pesticides draw their name from naturally occurring microscopic organisms, or microbes, that are used to control pests. In some cases, the pesticidal activity may derive from metabolites produced by these organisms.

The microbial category can be divided into six different kinds of pesticides:

Bacteria

This includes a variety of unicellular organisms with insecticidal and fungicidal properties. The ability to manufacture these organisms through industrial fermentation, as well as an ability to store them for extended periods, makes them ideal for use as biopesticides.

This subcategory is dominated by the species *Bacillus thuringiensis*, or Bt. Discovered in the early 20th century, Bts are bacteria that produce crystalline endotoxins, which disrupt digestive systems of many insect larvae. Used most commonly for control of Lepidopteran and Coleopteran pests, this group contains a number of subspecies that are ideal in that they provide highly specific control.

Fungi

Biorational fungi is a relatively new group of microbial products that surfaced in the 1980s and 90s. These fungi may display nematicidal, miticidal, insecticidal, fungicidal, and/or herbicidal properties. Like their bacterial counterparts, they can be manufactured through fermentation.

Weaknesses of some fungal products can include limited shelf life and dependence on favorable enviromental conditions for efficacy, as fungi need to grow in order to be effective. A significant amount of research is being devoted to improving the products in this subcategory.

Nematodes

Nematodes are used primarily for the control of insect larvae. The nematode worms enter the

VALENT BioSciences.
CORPORATION

insect through bodily openings and release bacteria which deliver a toxin that kills the host. Like fungi, nematodes can be affected adversely by unfavorable environmental conditions.

Protozoa

Protozoa are single-celled organisms which can act as cellular parasites. Currently, only one species of protozoa has been developed for commercial use: *Nosema locustae*, which provides grasshopper, locust, and cricket control on rangeland.

Viruses

Another form of bioinsecticides, viruses are described as intracellular parasites. Viruses are highly specific non-living organisms that consist of DNA or RNA material protected by a protein coat. When a virus comes in contact with a compatible host cell, the DNA or RNA material is injected into the cell's nucleus, where it causes reproduction of new viral particles. These particles then spread to additional host cells and can cause significant cellular damage and are vectors of disease.

Bioinsecticides derived from this subcategory include nuclear polyhedrosis viruses (NPVs) and granulosis viruses (GVs), and can be used to infect plant-harming insects such as armyworms and bollworms.

Yeast

Yeast microbials includes a small group of products to control postharvest pathogens that promote fruit decay. These products may also act by stimulating natural defense mechanisms in plants to help ward off disease.

Types of Microbial Pesticides and Targets

Type	Target
Bacteria	Fly and beetle larvae, caterpillars, fungal and bacterial diseases, soilborne pathogens
Fungi	Nematodes, whiteflies, aphids, thrips, beetles, locusts, grasshoppers, fungal diseases, soilborne pathogens, weeds
Nematodes	Beetle adults and larvae, grubs, caterpillars, flies, gnats, slugs
Protozoa	Grasshoppers, locusts, crickets
Viruses	Caterpillars
Yeast	Leaf spot, fruit drop, greasy spot

For the purposes of this guide, we will focus primarily on the bacterial class of microbial products. Accounting for between 80%-90% of all microbial pesticide product sales, bacteria are the least susceptible to changes in environmental conditions, and are the most widely adapted to mainstream commercial agriculture.

Five Reasons to Use Microbial Products

On the surface, microbial products bring the same fundamental benefit as any other agricultural pesticide; they kill pests that damage crops. But like all biorational products, microbials bring added value through a series of unique benefits, usually in a program where they work in conjunction with traditional chemicals.

Typically, growers who use microbial products are seeking to gain one or more of the following benefits:

1 Resistance Management Benefits
Extending the life of their traditional products

2 Residue Management Benefits
Food Quality Protection Act (FQPA) compliance and food safety benefits

3 Products Approved for Organic Production
The mainstay of organic pest control

4 Integrated Pest Management Tool
Highly selective, and safe for beneficials

5 Return on Investment
Microbials reduce total program cost. Bottom-line improvement is realized through all of the above.

VALENT BIOSCIENCES.
CORPORATION

Five Reasons to Use Microbial Products
Products Approved For Organic Production

3

In the consumer realm, microbial products are perhaps best known for their role in the production of organic foods. Products must meet regionally accepted organic standards, and certification is an integral part of that process. Many, but not all, biorational products meet the standards set forth by certifying agencies.

In fact, it's safe to say that without microbial pesticides, the organic industry would be hard pressed to compete in today's market. As environmentally friendly and naturally occuring organisms, microbial pesticides provide organic growers with powerful crop protection tools that take the place of synthetic chemicals. When applied correctly, these products can perform as well as their traditional counterparts.

Once again, this benefit translates into marketing advantages through organic labeling and branding. Consumers, particularly in the U.S. and Western Europe, have demonstrated that they're willing to pay a premium for organic foods. In recent years, this phenomenon has led many conventional farmers to convert a portion of their acreage to organic production.

Five Reasons to Use Microbial Products
Integrated Pest Management Tool

4

Public policy makers are growing more assertive in their encouragement of responsible pesticide use. Integrated Pest Management, or IPM, is a broad concept most commonly associated with these strategic pest control tactics (see sidebar).

When designing a comprehensive plan that considers all options to control pest problems, microbial products emerge as a low-risk, highly effective tool for achieving crop protection goals. IPM encompasses many of the aforementioned benefits of biorational use, benefits such as resistance management and compatibility with traditional chemistries. And as a prime example of environmentally-friendly product category that works well on a large scale, microbial insecticides have become cornerstones of IPM programs throughout the world.

Research, field trials, and performance history have proven the effectiveness of microbial products. Tests have shown that Bts won't harm bees, birds, fish or other wildlife. Studies have also shown that they won't harm beneficial insects that help keep secondary insects in check. All of these factors combine to make microbials a mainstay for IPM.

What is IPM?

The concept of Integrated Pest Management (IPM) involves a combination of practices that seek to:
- combine cultural, biological, and chemical means to control pests
- minimize economic, public health, and environmental risks in the process.

IPM is not a new concept. Introduced in the late 1960s, the heart of an IPM program lies in the complex system of checks and balances that make implementation a sound economic choice. It centers around strategies and tactics that involve competing factors; and biorationals help bridge that gap. How?

Biorationals:
- are an ideal partner for traditional chemicals, managing resistance and environmental impact;
- work best in combination with cultural pest control practices, mitigating economic impact;
- are nontoxic to humans and beneficials;
- are a proven and effective pest management tool that achieves each of these goals while managing risk.

Understanding Biorational Products

Five Reasons to Use Microbial Products
Return on Investment

5

Growers experienced in the use of microbial products know that economic benefits are realized through a combination of factors, some of which are long-term benefits based on keeping other pest control options viable.

Microbials offer a return on investment through the following means:

- Provide narrowly targeted pest control options;

- Which in turn, helps maintain or maximize beneficial populations;

- Helps prevent development of resistance to traditional chemicals;

- Helps bring back traditional chemicals lost to resistance;

- Prolongs the life of selective new chemistries, which are highly prone to resistance;

- Are typically as cost-effective as most conventional products;

- Combining all factors can reduce total crop protection costs.

Bacillus thuringiensis (Bt)

What is Bt?

Bacillus thuringiensis, or Bt, is a rod-shaped, spore-forming microorganism found throughout most of the world. It occurs naturally in soil and on leaves and other environmental settings. Thousands of strains of Bt bacteria exist, and a few of these have been identified and used to manufacture microbial insecticides. Harmless to human beings, birds and other animals, Bt is lethal to hundreds of species of insects when ingested. Just as traditional chemicals can be highly targeted, different strains of Bts show specificity to different pests. This provides growers with an effective and selective tool for use on a wide range of destructive pests on host crops.

Selectivity

Because different bacterial protein toxins are more active against certain insects than others, the key to effective, broad spectrum control is having a blend of multiple toxins. Whereas many biological products exist that have just a single toxin or low levels of two or three toxins, VBC's Bt products contain multiple toxins to maximize pest control.

Spores

Not all Bt products contain spores, but the highest quality Bt products do. Scientists have shown that bacterial spores greatly enhance pesticidal properties. The spores germinate within the insect and allow the bacteria to take over its body tissues, turning the insect into "a bag of Bts" and accelerating the kill.

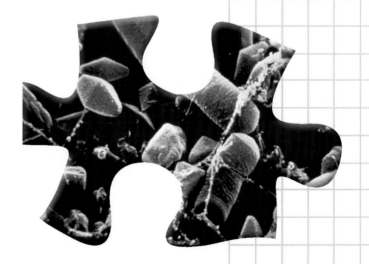

VALENT BIOSCIENCES CORPORATION

How Bts Work

You do not have to be a scientist to use Bts effectively or to understand how they work.

Bts contain protein endotoxin crystals and living spores. With insect populations, the protein endotoxin acts as a selective stomach poison. Spores contribute to their toxicity by causing blood poisoning and providing environmental persistence.

When an insect pest ingests the crystal proteins from treated leaves, feeding stops within minutes after the crystals are solubilized in the gut and gut cells are damaged. After toxin damage to the gut occurs, spores enter through the gut wall and germinate rapidly in the body cavity causing blood poisoning. Larvae stop feeding within minutes and die in 1-3 days. The affected larvae move slowly, discolor, then shrivel, blacken, and die. Smaller larvae die more quickly, which suggests that precise timing can measurably improve the performance of the application.

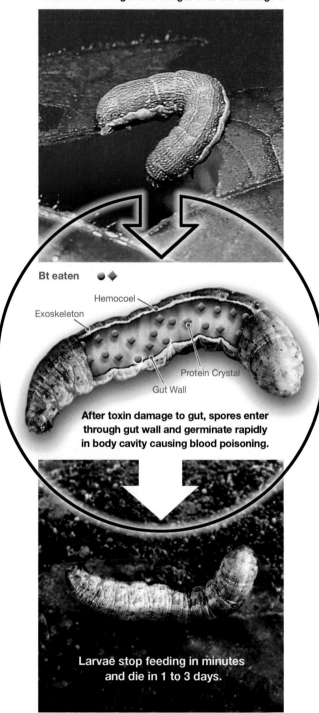

Ingestion of Bt's crystal proteins from treated leaves. Feeding stops within minutes after crystals are solubilized in the gut and the gut cells are damaged.

Bt eaten

Hemocoel
Exoskeleton
Protein Crystal
Gut Wall

After toxin damage to gut, spores enter through gut wall and germinate rapidly in body cavity causing blood poisoning.

Larvae stop feeding in minutes and die in 1 to 3 days.

Bt kurstaki (DiPel)®

Bt *kurstaki* (Btk) is a subspecies of *Bacillus thuringiensis*, and is the most frequently used biological insecticide in the world. In most markets, Btk is known more commonly as the VBC brand DiPel, the number-one selling Bt product worldwide.

Used on more than 200 different crops, including vegetables, fruit, nuts, vines, cotton, and corn, DiPel offers proven, cost-effective, broad spectrum worm control on 55 species of lepidopteran pests. Used as a tank-mix or as a rotation partner with other insecticides, DiPel is an especially integral tool in many insect resistance management programs.

Another key benefit of Btk is its status as a nonrestricted use pesticide. It does not require a restricted use permit for either purchase or use, and can be applied up to the time of harvest (although regional regulations may vary and should be consulted for allowable preharvest intervals). This feature makes DiPel perfect for late-season applications.

Success Factors when using DiPel

When applied properly, DiPel is a powerful insect management tool. As with any other pesticides, proper application is key to realizing the expected benefits. For success with DiPel products:

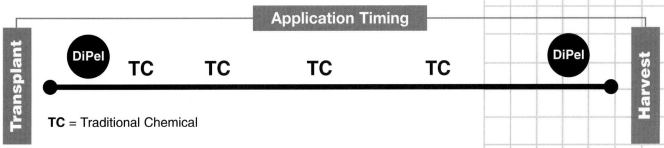

TC = Traditional Chemical

Most growers experienced in the use of DiPel have incorporated it into their standard program with specific benefits in mind. DiPel offers a price advantage and high kill rate in the early season while infestation levels are low, and also helps maintain beneficial populations. Traditional chemicals maintain a clean field and increase the spectrum of activity mid-season. With an application prior to harvest, DiPel brings the benefit of clean crops at packout, the lowest possible preharvest interval, minimized chemical residue, and diverse modes of action to maximize the product life cycle.

VALENT BIOSCIENCES CORPORATION

UNDERSTANDING MICROBIALS

■ Larvae must be actively feeding on treated, exposed plant surfaces.

■ Close scouting and early attention to infestations is highly recommended.

■ Thorough spray coverage is needed to provide a uniform deposit at the site of larval feeding.

■ Apply by conventional ground or air equipment, as well as sprinkler chemigation systems.

■ Use of a spreader-sticker or surfactant, which has been approved for use on growing and harvested crops, is recommended, especially on hard-to-wet crops like cabbage.

■ Apply before economic thresholds of damage have been exceeded.

■ Avoid applications during periods of cold or excessively hot temperatures.

The DiPel Family

As VBC's Bt *kurstaki* product, DiPel, is recommended and used by more growers and consultants than any other biological insecticide.

DiPel® Biobit®

DiPel technology relies on a potent bacterial strain that produces five bacterial protein toxins for broad spectrum vegetable worm control, including cabbage looper, armyworm, diamondback moth, *Helicoverpa*, imported cabbageworm, and other Lepidoptera. The balanced blend of toxins (CryIAa, CryIAb, CryIAc, CryIIA, CryIIB) and a spore, enhance efficacy and assist in resistance management. DiPel is also known as Biobit® in select markets,

Strict quality control standards ensure high-quality products and unsurpassed field performance.

VBC offers *Bacillus thuringiensis* spp. *kurstaki* products in a variety of easy to use formulations to meet grower needs.

DiPel DF	DiPel WP
DiPel 2x	Biobit HP
DiPel ES	Biobit XL
DiPel Pro DF	

History of Microbial Insecticides at VBC

Valent BioSciences has been involved in developing microbial insecticides from the start. Formerly part of Abbott Laboratories, Valent BioSciences led the early research and development efforts that resulted in commercially available Bt products. The company is the world leader in the research, development, formulation, marketing, and application of Bt-based biological insecticides.

The first commercial use of Bt in the U.S. occurred in 1958. During the 1960s, several trial formulations were developed and, in 1972, Abbott Laboratories introduced DiPel, the world's leading biological insecticide, based on the Bt *kurstaki* strain. This product innovation was driven by three primary factors: resistant insects; toxic pesticide residues; and worker re-entry. At this time, scientists had also determined that Bt showed specificity against caterpillar species in the order Lepidoptera.

The introduction of synthetic pyrethroids slowed the development of Bts somewhat, but insects began developing resistance to pyrethroids and, in the 1980s, many growers returned to biorationals and IPM programs.

In 1983, the scope of Bt coverage increased when scientists first published papers on the Bt *tenebrionis* strain, with observed activity against some beetles in the order Coleoptera. Each new strain that has been discovered demonstrates new levels of specificity, proving that Bts are ideal for IPM programs and environmentally sensitive uses.

Bt continues to be the most widely used biopesticide in the world, accounting for more than 90% of all commercial sales.

In January 2000, Sumitomo Chemical Company acquired the Ag Specialties Business of Abbott Laboratories. As Abbott Laboratories and now as Valent BioSciences Corporation, we have spent over 40 years developing environmentally friendly products for agriculture markets throughout the world. Today, Sumitomo Chemical is the leader in selling biorational products alongside their traditional products.

VALENT BIOSCIENCES.
CORPORATION

Bt aizawai (XenTari)®

Another subspecies of Bt, Bt *aizawai* (Bta) also provides exceptionally effective microbial control for key pests such as armyworms and diamondback moth larvae.

Known most commonly as the VBC product XenTari, Bta controls worms on vegetables, fruits, nuts, row crops, and turf, and has become a cornerstone product in IPM programs. A particularly common application of XenTari is being used as a rotation partner with DiPel, for an all biological resistance management program.

XenTari is also particularly effective against diamondback moth, a pest notorious for its adaptivity and ability to develop resistance quickly. It can be used alone, may be tank-mixed, or rotated with other effective insecticides.

Using XenTari

Like DiPel, proper application of XenTari is key to realizing the expected benefits. For success with XenTari:

■ Apply when early instar larvae are actively feeding before crop damage occurs.

■ Larvae must be feeding on exposed plant surfaces.

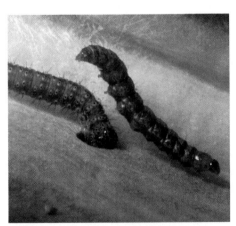

■ Thorough spray coverage is essential. Use sufficient spray volume to ensure uniform coverage without runoff.

■ Apply by conventional ground or air equipment, as well as sprinkler chemigation systems.

■ Use of spreader/stickers is recommended, especially on hard-to-wet crops like cabbage.

XenTari is particularly effective against diamondback moth, a pest notorious for being highly adaptive and developing resistance to chemical insecticides quickly.

XenTari and Florbac®

VBC's Bt *aizawai* product XenTari is the only natural biological insecticide based on the potent aizawai strain. Also known as Florbac in some markets, the technology includes five toxins and a spore, making it a particularly powerful resistance management tool.

XenTari and Florbac are widely used as effective controls for armyworm and diamondback moth larvae. In fact, XenTari is the only biological insecticide used for armyworm control more often than several traditional chemical brands.

VALENT BIOSCIENCES. CORPORATION

Myths about Potency

A key difference between microbial pesticides and traditional chemicals is how the active ingredient is measured. In traditional chemicals, that measure is defined as the percentage of pure active ingredient present in the product. With microbial products, the material being measured is from a fermentation process, and the analytical method is bioassay.

Unfortunately, several misconceptions surround the way that potency is defined.

Common myths about potency:
- Potency is the same as percent active in a chemical *(false)*.
- Potency is an indicator of field efficacy *(false)*.
- Potency can be used to compare one product with another *(false)*.
- Potency can be used to determine rates in the field *(false)*.
- Potency measures effectiveness on all labeled pests *(false)*.
- Potency is calculated the same way by every company *(false)*.
- The same procedures and pests are used to calculate potency for every company *(false)*.

Potency tells how much of the product is necessary to kill the target pest. But without exception, that value is specific both to the target pest and the company that produces the product. Not only does potency vary from insect to insect, but every manufacturer uses different parameters and processes when calculating potency.

It follows that these values cannot be used relative to application rates for competing products. In other words, if the label for product "A" lists a potency of 10,000 Cabbage Looper Units (CLU/mg) and another lists a potency of 50,000 *Spodoptera exigua* Units (SEU/mg), comparing the two is like comparing apples and oranges.

Bt tenebrionis (Novodor)®

Bt *tenebrionis* (Novodor®), or Btt, is an insecticide based on the *tenebrionis* bacterial strain, used to control beetle pests such as the Colorado potato beetle (CPB). CPB is a ravenous pest that if left unchecked, can cause significant damage to potato, tomato, and eggplant crops.

Novodor also provides effective control of elm leaf beetle on ornamentals.

With a unique mode of action and distinct toxin profile, Novodor provides excellent control of selected Coleoptera pests, and like other Bts, is common in resistance management programs.

Using Novodor

■ Due to its unique mode of action, Novodor must be ingested by the target insect larvae to be effective. Therefore, thorough coverage of the crop to be protected is essential for best results. Upon ingestion, the protein is activated under the specific gut conditions of the target insect causing general gut paralysis and cessation of feeding within hours. Death occurs in 1-3 days.

■ While Novodor is formulated to provide desirable coverage and adherence to crop surfaces, additional adjuvants, spreaders, or stickers may be added to improve product performance, especially under rainy conditions or heavy dew. Avoid application if rainfall is imminent.

■ Novodor may be applied by ground or aerial equipment with sufficient quantities of water to provide thorough coverage of plant parts to be protected.

■ When larvae and adult beetles are present, an effective adulticide with rapid knock-down activity should be used.

VALENT BIOSCIENCES. CORPORATION

Evaluating Microbial Products

When considering using Bts or distinguishing between competitive products, what factors should you look for?

VBC Product ☑️ **Efficacy Must be a Given**

To realize the benefits from any microbial product, consistent pesticidal activity has to be the starting point. Effective and consistent field performance is the pathway to other market advantages microbial products bring. If you're not sure a product will work, any residual benefits are inconsequential.

VBC Product ☑️ **Quality Must be a Given**

Product quality means a product that is free of contaminants that can cause unwanted effects, such as phytotoxicity. Valent BioSciences translates its pharmaceutical grade quality standards into performance in the field.

VBC Product ☑️ **Bts Provide Selective Pest Control**

Used alone or in combination or rotation with traditional insecticides, Bts will control specific pests in your field. Through the selectivity of Bt toxins, some Bts show specificity to caterpillar species in the order Lepidoptera, while others target beetles in the order Coleoptera. Seek advice on the product that's right for your crop and your pest problems.

VBC Product ☑️ **Formulation Choice and Ease of Use**

To enjoy the advantages of Bt technology, one needs a formulation that makes the product easy to use. Always choose products that come in a number of formulations to suit a variety of cropping, pests, application equipment, environmental conditions, user preference, and cost requirements.

VBC Product ☑️ **Dependable Product Support**

A grower who invests in microbial products should have access to a highly trained sales and technical staff with a history of personalized, long-term commitment to customer service.

VBC Product ☑️ **Economics Make Sense**

Of course, cost is a critical factor in a grower's decision to purchase inputs. The bottom line is that when used correctly, Bt products ensure a return on investment by reducing total costs. Pest populations are controlled, while beneficial levels are maintained. Sprays may be reduced. Other products last longer. And most importantly, crops thrive and market windows are opened.

Nematicides

Nematodes represent one of the most damaging pest complexes that attack plants. These microscopic roundworms feed on and in the roots, severely damaging or killing them.

The objective in nematode management is to protect the plant from nematode damage, allowing for healthy root development, efficient uptake of nutrients and water, optimum plant growth, and sustainable economical yields. Unfortunately for growers, traditional fumigants used to control nematodes, such as methyl bromide, are being phased out.

VBC answered this challenge by developing an environmentally responsible microbial nematicide as an alternative to traditional products. DiTera® provides protection through three direct modes of action: by killing nematodes on contact through paralysis of the feeding mechanism; by causing disorientation of nematodes by affecting their neurotransmitters resulting in starvation; and by preventing egg hatching and development.

Yet equally important is an indirect benefit gained through use of DiTera. Studies show that the product significantly enhances beneficial microbe populations, reducing susceptibility to secondary infections leading to improved plant vigor. Root mass increase is often dramatic, resulting in yield enhancement.

VALENT BioSciences CORPORATION

Myrothecium verrucaria (DiTera)®

DiTera is the leader in microbial nematicides in today's market, and is manufactured using the microorganism *Myrothecium verrucaria*. This product selectively controls plant parasitic nematodes that affect the root systems of many economic crops, such as grapes, pineapples, nut crops, stone fruit, citrus, bananas, cole crops, tomatoes, turf, and ornamentals.

The technology is based on a simple concept: Root health leads to productivity. It follows that the best way to measure the benefits of DiTera is through yield, root development, and plant vigor.

Unlike assessments for traditional nematicides, standard soil extraction methods for nematode counts may not accurately measure the effects of DiTera for two reasons: First, soil extraction does not differentiate paralyzed or weakened nematodes from actively feeding parasites. This means that nematode counts measured from soil extraction will include those that are living but can no longer harm the plant.

The second reason is the observed effect of DiTera application on the root systems of healthy plants. Studies show that DiTera promotes root growth and may significantly increase root mass, meaning that the ratio of

nematodes to root density is measurably lower (see DiTera's Indirect Benefits).

Using DiTera

DiTera can be used at planting or in existing plots where the soil is infested with nematodes. It may be applied to the soil as a pre-plant, at planting or post-plant treatment on annual and perennial crops.

DiTera is also one of the only products that can be applied as a sidedress around already established plants. There are no restrictions on the number of annual applications with multiple root flushes.

DiTera's Indirect Benefits

The increase of soil microbial populations is a pronounced benefit of DiTera application. Collaborative research shows that increased microbial populations — especially in the rhizosphere — results in a similar increase in catalase, protease, chitiobiase, and urease activities. This increased enzyme activity is consistent across multiple soil types, and brings about visible changes in root mass density.

Since its introduction in 1996, DiTera has become an especially valuable tool in high quality wine growing regions in the Americas. In the Napa Valley region of the U.S., yield increases versus untreated plots consistently measure in excess of 15%. In Chile, where *Xiphenima* pressure is high, adoption of the technology is also becoming the standard.

Similarly, adoption in vegetable fields is becoming more common as increased root mass is resulting in significant yield — and profit — enhancements. Tomato and pepper growers, particularly, have been quick to adopt the technology.

Pictured here are cutaway views showing root system development from DiTera-treated (top) and traditional chemical- treated (bottom) bell pepper plots in Sinaloa, Mexico (2002-2003). The marked increase in root density from this trial, promoting greater nutrient uptake and plant vigor, resulted in a yield increase of nearly 1000 crates/ha versus the grower standard.

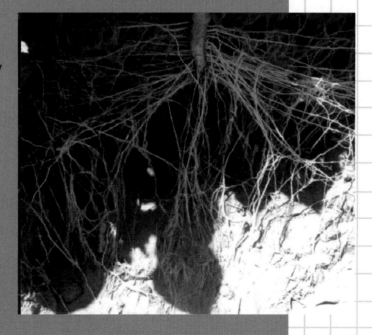

VALENT BIOSCIENCES. CORPORATION

Understanding PGRs

Understanding Biorational Products – Plant Growth Regulators (PGRs)

Comprised of naturally occurring hormones and man-made, synthesized compounds, plant growth regulators (PGRs) can promote, inhibit or modify the physiological traits of a variety of fruit, vegetable, and other agronomic crops. This powerful ability allows PGRs to maximize a crop's own genetic potential — optimizing yield, crop quality, and overall grower returns.

In some markets, the effects of PGRs are so critical that they are applied to virtually 100% of the acreage in production. Yet one of the most interesting aspects of these products is that use patterns, objectives for use, and expected benefits often vary from market to market. This is because growing conditions and/or market windows can be dramatically different from region to region.

Through applications linked to specific stages of the plant growth cycle, PGRs allow growers to manipulate variables that can maximize return on investment. These variables can, for example, impact fruit quality by affecting fruit set, size, color, harvest time, and shelf life. PGRs can also be used to improve crop management activities such as timing of herbicides and fertilizers, or the harvest operation.

Yet all PGRs are not the same. The effectiveness and consistency of these products depend on quality control during manufacturing as well as formulation technology.

VALENT BioSciences.
CORPORATION

Five Major Classes of Plant Hormones

Natural hormones are divided into the following five major classes, each with very specific and important roles:

Auxins

■ Auxins play a role in cell enlargement, cell division, vascular tissue differentiation, root initiation, tropic responses, apical dominance, leaf senescence, leaf and fruit abscission, fruit setting and growth, assimilate partitioning, fruit ripening, flowering, growth of flower parts, promotion of femaleness in dioecious flowers.

Gibberellins (GA's)

■ Gibberellins play a role in cell elongation, stem growth, bolting in long-day plants, induction of seed germination, enzyme production during germination, fruit setting and growth, induction of maleness in dioecious flowers.

Cytokinins

■ Cytokinins are involved in cell division, morphogenesis, growth of lateral buds, leaf expansion, delay of leaf senescence, enhancement of stomatal opening, chloroplast development.

Abscisic Acid (ABA)

■ ABA can influence stomatal closure, inhibition of shoot growth, induction of synthesis of storage proteins in seeds, inhibits gibberellin-induced alpha-amylase synthesis in seeds, affects seeds dormancy, involved in plant defense mechanisms against wounding by pathogens.

Ethylene

■ Ethylene can perform stimulation of lateral growth in stems, maintenance of the apical hook in seedlings, stimulation of defense responses to injury, release from dormancy, shoot and root growth and differentiation, adventitious root formation, leaf and fruit abscission, induction of flowering, induction of femaleness in dioecious flowers, flower opening, flower leaf and senescence, fruit ripening.

Other Plant Compounds with Suggested PGR Activity

Polyamines

■ Polyamines are involved in cell division and morphogenesis. They interact with ethylene functions in maturation, ripening, and senescence.

Brassinosteroids

■ These compounds affect cell division, cell elongation, vascular differentiation. They are involved in fertility, inhibition of root growth and development, promotion of ethylene synthesis and epinasty.

Jasmonates

■ Jasmonates play a role in plant defense through induction of synthesis of proteinase inhibitors, inhibition of plant growth and seed germination, promotion of senescence, abscission, tuber formation, fruit ripening, pigment formation.

Salicylic Acid

■ Salicylic Acid promotes resistance to pathogens by induction of synthesis of specific proteins, causes thermogenesis in Arum flowers, enhancement of flower longevity, inhibition of seed germination and ethylene synthesis, blocking of the wound response, and reverses the effects of ABA.

Signal Peptides

■ Signal peptides activate defense responses and cell proliferation in cell cultures. They help determine cell fate during the development of the apical meristem, modulation of root growth and leaf patterning in the presence of auxin and cytokinin, peptide signaling for self-compatibility, and symbiotic nodule formation in legumes.

UNDERSTANDING PGRs

Major Commercial PGRs and their Effect/Benefit

PGR Effect/Benefit	Examples of Commercial PGRs
Growth promotion	Auxins, Gibberellins, Cytokinins, Folcisteine, Forchlorfenuron, 4-CPA
Growth retardation	Mepiquat Chloride, Prohexadione-Ca, Ancymidol, Flurprimidol, Chlormequat, Dikegulac-sodium, Mefluidide, Uniconazole, Paclobutrazol, Trinexapac-ethyl, Maleic Hydrazide in tobacco, Chlorflurenol-methyl
Growth inhibition	Fatty acids
Fruit thinning	1-Naphthaleneacetic Acid (NAA), 1-Naphthaleneacetamide, Carbaryl, 6-Benzyladenine (6BA), Ethychlozate, Sulfocarbamide, Ethephon
Dormancy breaking	Hydrogen Cyanamide, Thiadiazuron, Mineral Oils
Prolongs dormancy	ABA
Ripening agents	Ethylene, Ethephon, Glyphosate*, Glyphosine
Flower bud induction	Ethylene, Ethephon, NAA, Gibberrelic Acid (GA3)
Stimulation of return bloom	6BA, NAA, Ethrel
Suppression of return bloom	GA3, GA7
Delay ripening	GA, Aminoethoxyvinylglycine (AVG), Methylcyclopropene (MCP), Daminozide
Suppression of potato sprouting	Chlorpropham
Promotion of branching	6BA, Ciclanilide, Triiodobenzoic Acid
Reduce pre-harvest fruit drop	AVG, NAA, Daminozide, 2,4-D, 2,4,5-TP, Dichloroprop
Defoliants	Ethephon, Thidiazuron, Dimethipin, Tribufos
Fruit and nut loosening for mechanical harvest	Ethephon
Replaces cold requirement for flowering	GA3
Stimulate seed germination	GA3, GA47, Ethephon
Delay fruit maturation and senescence	AVG, GA3, 6BA, MCP
Reduce post-harvest physiological disorders	AVG (for watercore and greasiness), DPA and Ethoxyquin (for superficial scald)
Increase sugars in fruits	Ethephon, Ethychlozate
Promotes rooting of cuttings for asexual propagation	IBA
Reduce suckering in tobacco	Ethephon, Fatty Alcohols, Maleic Hydrazide
Induce flowering in pineapple	Ethephon, Ethylene
Promotes ripening and degreening	Ethylene

list includes traditional chemicals marketed for PGR effects

VALENT BIOSCIENCES.
CORPORATION

Gibberellins
GA3 (Gibberellic Acid)

Gibberellic acid, or GA3, is a plant growth regulator found naturally in virtually all plant species. Gibberellic acid is primarily a very potent growth promotant — increasing size and quality of fruits, vegetables and other crops — but also playing a key role in the regulation of other plant processes such as flowering, seed germination, dormancy and senescence. ProGibb®, from VBC, is the most widely used and most commonly known GA3 product in the world*. It is used to increase yields and improve quality on table grapes, citrus, cherries and many other fruits and vegetables and agronomic crops, and also improve germination and stimulate early growth on rice.

History of
Plant Growth Regulators at VBC

Agricultural researchers first recognized the true value of plant growth regulators as early as the 1930s. Since that time, a wide variety of both natural and synthetic compounds have been discovered and developed.

Valent BioSciences, then working as Abbott Laboratories, entered the PGR development arena in 1957 and quickly assumed a lead role with the introduction of ProGibb in 1962. ProGibb remains the most widely used plant growth regulator in commercial agriculture today.

With intense research worldwide in the 1960s and 1970s, effects of PGRs were documented on more than 50 crops. Valent BioSciences introduced the powerful new PGR, Promalin®. It has since become one of the most widely adopted plant growth regulators around the world.

At VBC, PGR history has been rich with product developments and technical acquisitions over the course of 40 years. From ProGibb to its newest PGR (Prestige)™ product launched in 2005, VBC remains dedicated to creating value and providing solutions for its customers around the world. The company remains the worldwide leader in the identification, market assessment, development, registration and marketing of PGRs.

* Valent BioSciences Corporation's GA3 (gibberellic acid) is sold, around the world, under the brands names ProGibb®, Activol®, Berelex®, Release®, RyzUp®, and Accel®.

Major Commercial Uses of ProGibb

Crop	Physiological Effect	Benefits
Table grapes	Cell division and cell growth, stem elongation, berry thinning	Improves berry size, cluster quality, and packout.
Citrus fruits	Delays senescence	Improves rind quality, prolongs harvest season.
Citrus fruits	Causes parthenocarpic fruit set	Increases fruit set in hybrid mandarines.
Sweet cherry	Extends growth cycle, postpones the end of the maturation period	Improves fruit size, firmness, color, and overall quality. Allow for shipping to long distances without losing quality.
Sour cherry	Overcomes cherry yellow virus. Mechanism not fully understood	Reinvigorates affected trees, promotes vegetative growth and flower bud formation, restores sustainable production.
Spinach and leafy vegetables	Cell division and expansion	Makes leaves erect to facilitate and optimize mechanical harvest. Also increases leaf size and yield.
Rice seed treatment	Stimulates seed germination	Accelerates seedling emergence, stand establishment, and permanent flood. Improves crop management.
Seed potatoes	Replaces dormancy requirements	Allows for planting and sprouting potato seed right after harvest.
Banana	Promotion of cell growth under adverse conditions. Delays fruit maturation	Overcomes low temperature stress, increases fruit size and packout. As a postharvest treatment extends green life.
Pineapple	Promotes cell division and expansion during early fruit growth. Delays senescence of the crown	Increases fruit size and packout. Maintains the crown green and fresh during transit and retail display.
Cotton	Promotes early cell division and stem elongation during adverse growing conditions	Accelerates plant growth during the "lag" phase, advances flower bud development and early boll set.
Lemons postharvest	Delays senescence, maintains rind integrity	Delays degreening during storage. Protects against sour rot attacks.
Cut flowers	Delays senescence	Extends vase life.
Hybrid Rice	Panicle exertion	Increase seed yield.
Pastures	Promote plant growth	Increase yields.

VALENT BioSciences. CORPORATION

ProGibb Applications: Table Grapes

The use of GA3 in table grapes started in the late 50s with the advent of seedless varieties. Seedless berries remain very small because the seed is the site where gibberellins and other hormones are produced. The spraying of GA3 to 1) stretch the cluster, 2) thin the berries, and 3) enlarge the berries made it possible for these varieties to become a commercial reality.

Today, ProGibb is a must to grow quality table grapes. The use of GA3 in seedless table grapes started in California and then spread to all major table grape-producing areas: Chile, Mexico, South Africa, Australia, and the Mediterranean countries. Today, a great deal of basic and applied knowledge has been developed in all those markets. Product use varies slightly from region to region and from variety to variety as climatic conditions, soils, etc., change, but the main objective of producing a high quality grape is the same everywhere. With time, the use of GA3 expanded to seeded table grape varieties. Even though those varieties have seeds, they also benefit from GA3 treatments to enlarge the cluster, thin the berries, and increase cluster uniformity, berry size, and quality.

Bottom line
IMPACT:

As ProGibb treatments are standard practice to grow table grapes, it is difficult to place a value on its contribution to the overall value of the crop at harvest. Most table grapes not treated with GA3 would not be salable. The price that table grape growers get for their product is mainly affected by berry size, berry size uniformity (absence of small berries), berry firmness, and uniform color. How well the fruit holds up during storage, transit, and during retail display is also critical, and buyers keep detailed records of these attributes in shipments coming from different producers. It is not uncommon to see differences in prices per box of $1, $3, and up to $5, based only on fruit quality and visual appearance. So for a grower packing 800 boxes to the acre, a difference of $3 per box may represent $2,400 of incremental income per acre. This superior quality is obtained in part by carrying out a well-designed ProGibb spray program, and may be perceived as being expensive by those unfamiliar with table grape production costs. In reality, the ProGibb program costs only a fraction of the incremental return per acre.

VALENT BioSciences.
CORPORATION

ProGibb Applications: Sour Cherry

In the United States, more than 90% of sour cherries are grown in Michigan. A major problem there is Cherry "Yellows" Virus, which makes the fruiting buds fall off leaving bare branches, or "blind wood."

In the 70s, Dr. John M. Bukovac of Michigan State University found that applications of GA3 early in the spring significantly reduced the incidence of the disease, and if applied yearly, allowed trees to recover and become very productive again. As a result, total production of sour cherry has increased significantly because growers were able to harvest much more fruit out of mature and old orchards.

Bottom line IMPACT:

Since the adoption of this application, the total area of sour cherry has decreased slightly, and yet total production has risen due to productivity increases. The industry has since regulated supply taking into account that less and less orchards are affected by the "Yellows" Virus.

ProGibb Applications: Spinach and Leafy Vegetables

A relatively small market, nonetheless, application on spinach provides an interesting example of a unique benefit derived from ProGibb.

Spinach is a leafy vegetable that grows very close to the ground. Most spinach is mechanically harvested, so harvest efficiency can be adversely affected by the cutting blade missing leaves or leaf parts, or by picking up clods.

A single application of ProGibb a few days prior to harvest will make the leaves stand up and become erect. Also, leaf blades grow more as a result of the treatment. This means the cutting blade can be raised, goes faster, and picks up more leaves and less dirt. On the second cut, the leaves grow in a more upright position and the blade can be easily placed right above the stumps from the first cut.

In countries with intense vegetable production such as Thailand, Vietnam, India, and Indonesia, ProGibb is used in many leafy vegetables to speed up growth, increase leaf size, and shorten the time to harvest. In these countries, land is limited, consumption of vegetables is very high, and growers raise several crops a year in the same piece of ground. Speeding up days to harvest can be extremely important.

Bottom line IMPACT:

The expected increase in revenue due to this treatment can be 10-30 times its cost depending on the crop, location, etc. This is without considering the value of shortening the crop cycle, obtaining a cleaner crop, etc.

VALENT BIOSCIENCES. CORPORATION

GA3 Applications: Release® Rice Seed Treatment

With the introduction of semi-dwarf varieties of rice in the US in the late 1980s, significant problems with seed germination and uniform stand establishment were encountered. The semi-dwarf varieties were created to reduce the loss of yield due to lodging. However, these varieties also had reduced endogenous gibberellins.

While this reduction in gibberellin content did not affect mature plant vigor, yield, or grain quality, it did affect the germination process. Low, delayed, and uneven germination resulted in lower yields and lower grain quality, the need to re-seed, and significant losses to the industry. VBC developed a gibberellin seed treatment (Release) to overcome this problem. The treatment has several significant benefits:

✔ Faster and more uniform germination;

✔ Faster and more uniform stand establishment;

✔ Reduction of the seedling rate;

✔ Allows the farmer to plant deeper and take advantage of soil moisture thus reducing costly temporary floods;

✔ Allows the farmer to plant earlier at somewhat lower soil temperatures;

✔ Advancement of the permanent flood date, thus achieving better weed control and in some cases, elimination of one herbicide spray.

✔ More uniform seed head emergence and seed maturity;

✔ Improvement of grain quality, with higher percentage of "wholes", thus reducing the percentage of "greens" and "brokens"; and

✔ Shortening of the growing season by up to three to seven days.

The Release seed treatment is combined with application of seed protectants. Seed can be treated anytime between harvest and planting date and stored. Since its introduction, Release's use has been extended to some tall (normal height) varieties that also benefit from the treatment. Different varieties respond similarly to the treatment, with more vigorous varieties requiring a slightly lower rate. The current products and application procedures have given satisfactory results and their commercial adoption was immediate. Fifteen years after its introduction, commercial use of Release continues to be very strong for the varieties suitable to the treatment.

Bottom line
IMPACT:

A small investment has tremendously positive consequences for these growers. The main economic benefits for this treatment are:

■ Reduced need to flush the fields and provide additional moisture deeper, where seeds are planted. This can be extremely expensive.

■ Increased effectiveness of post-emergence herbicides as plants are very uniform in size and application timing can be optimized.

■ More uniform grain development, grain maturity, less greens, less brokens, less shedding of over dry grains in the field.

ProGibb Applications: Seed Potatoes

Most potato varieties must undergo a dormancy period of three to four months before they can be planted and sprout normally. In places where only one crop a year is planted, this is not a problem. In low latitudes, two or more crops can be planted. Seed potato from one harvest cannot be immediately planted. A treatment of ProGibb by spraying, dipping, or dusting, can replace the need for the dormant period and potatoes can be planted literally the day after they are dug.

Another application of this technique is in both seed production and seed breeding

programs. When breeding or seed production programs are being conducted in different hemispheres, the seed can be harvested and planted right away after treatment.

Bottom line IMPACT:

This technique saves lots of money in having to either buy seed from other sources or save and keep seed from a previous harvest (more than three to four months earlier). It is also a great tool for breeding programs, where they can grow generations back to back in greenhouses, etc.

ProGibb Applications: Tropical Fruits

ProGibb has demonstrated significant benefits for growers of bananas and pineapples.

The most important effect of ProGibb on bananas is fruit size, particularly during the cooler months of the year where growing conditions are less than ideal and fruit size, yield and packout are reduced. Another interesting benefit of ProGibb on bananas is an aid in the control of the fungal disease Black Sigatoka — the world's biggest problem in banana production. Control of this pathogen can require 20-35 aerial fungicide applications per year, placing significant pressure on the plant foliage. ProGibb helps the foliage recover, specifically from the negative effects of using so many fungicide sprays. A third benefit for banana producers is GA3's ability to extend "green life" and improving shelf life for transit.

In pineapple, ProGibb has a major effect on fruit size, as applications of GA3 early in the development of the fruit will stimulate cell division and cell elongation. A second benefit is that a postharvest application to the crown of the fruit keeps the crown looking green and fresh, contributing handsomely to the eye-appeal of the fruit.

Bottom line IMPACT:

Improvement of fruit size results in higher prices. Better quality allows for shipping of fruit to far away markets and helps ensure the crop arrives in good condition.

VALENT BioSciences. CORPORATION

ProGibb Applications: Ornamental Crops and Turf

ProGibb has long been used to improve the quality and productivity of many ornamental crops. A few examples are:

■ Replacement of cold treatment to break dormancy in Azaleas;

■ Increases/advances flowering and/or increases flower size in Camelia, Geranium, Chrysanthemum, Spathiphyllum, and others;

■ Promotes stem elongation in many cut flower species such as Aster, Baby's Breath, Column Stock, Delphinium, Larkspur, and others;

■ Promotes faster vegetative growth in bedding plants.

In turf, ProGibb can improve the quality of turfgrass by improving greenness and reducing yellowing in golf courses and green spaces during the cool parts of the year where there is cold stress and frost damage. During warm weather, ProGibb can also enhance regrowth after mowing.

Bottom line IMPACT:

Productivity and consistently superior plant quality equals competitive advantage in the ornamental and turf markets, where eye appeal is even more critical than with food crops.

GA3 Applications: Cotton

In cotton, GA3 stimulates early growth while adding more leaf area, more nodes and more height for increased yield potential. It improves early season plant vigor and helps plants recover from stressful conditions caused by adverse weather (e.g., cool temperatures, wind and blowing sand, minor hail, and standing water) and other early season stresses such as thrips and other pest damage. The product can also help young cotton out of its early season lag growth phase.

Bottom line IMPACT:

In cotton production, the period of germination and early plant growth is critical. Ideally, the plant starts producing fruiting structures as early as possible as the bottom bolls are the most important to achieve high yields. GA3 application helps overcome "lag phase" in plant growth, a phase that can be aggravated by adverse weather, cool springs, wind, insects, or a host of other stresses. An application of GA3 can often make the difference between having to replant or not.

UNDERSTANDING PGRs

Gibberellins GA4 and GA7

Gibberellins are a large family of closely related natural hormones found in all plants. Scientists have numbered the gibberellins as they were found — *i.e.* GA1, GA2, etc. At this time, the number of different gibberellins identified in plants exceeds 100.

Not all these gibberellin compounds can be considered hormones. Many of these compounds are intermediates in the biochemical pathways of gibberellin synthesis, and as such may be highly unstable and/or may not have any hormonal action. Along with GA3, GA4 and GA7 are the only other gibberellins that have been developed for commercial use so far.

The mixture of GA4 plus GA7 (GA4+7) is produced by specific strains of the same fungus that produces GA3. VBC markets this mixture as ProVide®. At this time, the uses of GA4+7 are distinct but remain more limited than those for GA3. GA4+7 is used primarily in apples to improve fruit skin finish by reducing physiological russet, and to cause fruit size increase and fruit elongation (typiness). It also increases fruit set on pears.

VALENT BioSciences
CORPORATION

Gibberellins 4 and 7 Plus 6-Benzyladenine

GA4+7/6BA (Promalin®) is a mixture in equal parts of GA4+7 and 6-Benzyladenine. Again, different markets benefit from the attributes of this product in slightly different ways.

In the US, initially, the main use benefit was to improve fruit typiness and size in the Red Delicious variety. Now, Promalin is used in all main varieties to improve size. In Europe, the main objectives for using Promalin has been to control russet and for increasing fruit size. In Chile, it is used for fruit size and fruit finish. In South Africa, the product is combined with a thinner (NAD) to achieve fruit thinning, size increase, and russet control.

In Europe, they also use Promalin to increase fruit set in pears. Applied at bloom (from early bloom to late petal fall), the product causes fruit set and promotes cell division and cell elongation in the developing fruitlet. By harvest time, fruits that have more cells are bigger provided that the trees had adequate moisture and fertilizer during the growing season and that the tree was not overcropped. Promalin is also used to promote branching in nursery stock and in young trees in the orchard.

Bottom line IMPACT:

Promalin increases fruit size, yield, and packout. In addition, Promalin increases quality. In economic studies done over many years, it was found that Promalin can, on the average, increase yield by 6%, increase packout by shifting the size categories by half to one size, and shift a high percentage of the fruit into the highest quality category. In one study done over several years, the average incremental gross income fluctuated between $500 and $2000 per acre, with an investment in the treatment of a fraction of those amounts.

6-Benzyladenine

6-Benzyladenine (6BA) is a compound with cytokinin activity. Although 6BA is commercially synthesized for agricultural uses, 6BA can be considered a natural compound, as it has been found in nature in several organisms of the plant kingdom.

Over the years, 6BA has been used extensively as a branching agent in nursery stock and in ornamental plants. 6BA counteracts the apical dominance exerted by auxins, allowing the lateral latent buds to break and grow. This is critical in fruit trees to form an efficient canopy with many well-positioned scaffolds. It is also important in ornamental plants where a round, well-filled shape is desired and to avoid "leggy," misshapen plants.

Recently, VBC took the leadership to develop 6BA as a post-bloom thinning agent for apples. Since 1994, 6BA has been used as an apple thinner in many countries under the names Accel® and Cylex®. More recently, VBC developed MaxCel®, a second-generation 6BA thinner with improved action and very reliable performance. MaxCel increases fruit size beyond the thinning effect and ensures return bloom.

Additionally, MaxCel is being developed to improve yields in pistachio and to reduce the effects of alternate bearing.

VALENT BIOSCIENCES. CORPORATION

Aminoethoxyvinylglycine (ReTain)®

Aminoethoxyvinylglycine (AVG) is a natural compound produced by fermentation. AVG is a plant growth regulator that inhibits the biosynthesis of ethylene in plants. Ethylene is the natural plant hormone involved in fruit maturation, ripening, and abscission. AVG has been formulated and is commercialized under the brand name ReTain.

ReTain is a harvest management tool designed to help stone fruit growers realize the full potential value of their crop through the improvement and maintenance of fruit quality at harvest and after storage. Growers realize a variety of significant benefits, including:

■ Improved harvest management;

■ Reduced preharvest fruit drop;

■ Maintenance of fruit firmness;

■ Delay of starch degradation;

■ Delayed harvest that allows for natural increases in fruit size and color; and

■ Enhanced fruit storageability, including reduction of watercore, greasiness, and superficial scald.

Harvest Management

Harvest management is a broad term for a whole category of benefits. These benefits center around timing, allowing growers to delay harvest and harvest more fruit at optimum quality. In an operation with 500 acres of the same variety — with a 10-day harvest window at optimum maturity — labor, equipment, and cooling capacity become large considerations. ReTain can deliver an extra 7-10 days when applied, spacing out the crop and significantly increasing a grower's flexibility.

Stop Drop

An acre of apples can easily lose hundreds of bushels of apples due to preharvest drop. AVG significantly reduces fruit drop without allowing the fruit to soften. In many cases, stop drop impact alone recoups the grower's ReTain investment.

Increased Size

Retain treated fruit will mature slower so harvest date is delayed. Fruit on the tree can increase 1% of its weight per day. In 10 days time, the crop can be 10% larger (about 100 more boxes on the average), but more importantly the increase comes from the fruits being larger, not from adding more fruits. Larger fruits are worth more.

Fruit Set

It is well known that ethylene also plays a role during flowering and fruit set. In many species, fruit set can be limited by the abscission of flowers or small developing fruitlets due to the excessive production of ethylene by the plant at that time. This phenomenon has been demonstrated in walnut varieties susceptible to what is called Pistillate Flower Abortion, or PFA. In the walnut variety Serr, one application of ReTain at the beginning of the bloom period can double, triple, or even quadruple the amount of nut set, with the corresponding increase in nut yields and grower returns. Very possibly, similar benefits may be found in other nuts and fruit varieties.

Bottom line IMPACT:

Adding together two or three of the benefits listed above, growers can easily return $500-$2000/acre. And there are other benefits: Treated fruit stores better because it softens slower in storage.

VALENT BioSciences.

Understanding Your Supplier

Understanding Your Supplier
A Look at Manufacturing

The manufacturing processes for microbials and plant growth regulators are understood, but the quality of the end result is directly related to how precisely those processes are managed. A reliable, experienced supplier will deliver products that inspire confidence and bring added value to the crop.

Any manufacturing process involving living organisms requires a great deal of experience, skill, and stewardship throughout. Specialty crop producers and the professionals who advise them need to be confident that the products they use or recommend will perform consistently and reliably.

The manufacturing of microbial pesticides and PGRs involves a fermentation process combined with a post-fermentation product recovery stage. Given the number of critical variables involved, there are plenty of points where success depends on sophisticated management.

Fermentation:
A Look at the Process

The fermentation process works like this: A small quantity of the organism is placed in a "shake flask" in laboratory conditions with growth medium (a proprietary solution with the proper balance of nutrients to promote the growth of the bacterial culture).

Once the population builds to a sufficient level, the contents of the shake flask are transferred to a seed fermentor for further development, or directly to a large-scale production fermentor. During the process, the microorganism consumes the nutrients present and undergoes vegetative reproduction (cell division). This is what VBC wants to happen: for example, more cells mean more production of insecticidal proteins, which means a more potent and effective product since all of the production variables are managed properly.

In the case of Bt, once the fermentation is complete (typically a multi-day process), the batch is worked into a slurry concentrate by micro-filtration, evaporation, centrifuge, or a combination of techniques. The slurry is then dried and milled to form the technical powder, which provides the active ingredient for formulation. In the case of PGRs, the product then moves into a proprietary extraction/purification process.

Proprietary Process

The fermentation process at VBC is highly confidential and is the key to the quality and consistent performance of its products. The protein profile (the type, quantities, and proportions of insecticidal proteins present in the technical active ingredient) of Bt-based products are very different for different manufacturers. This is true even for products from the same subspecies of Bt, such as Btk. Modifications in the manufacturing process from one supplier to another will give each supplier's Btk product a different protein profile, resulting in different performance under field conditions.

FERMENTATION PROCESS FLOW

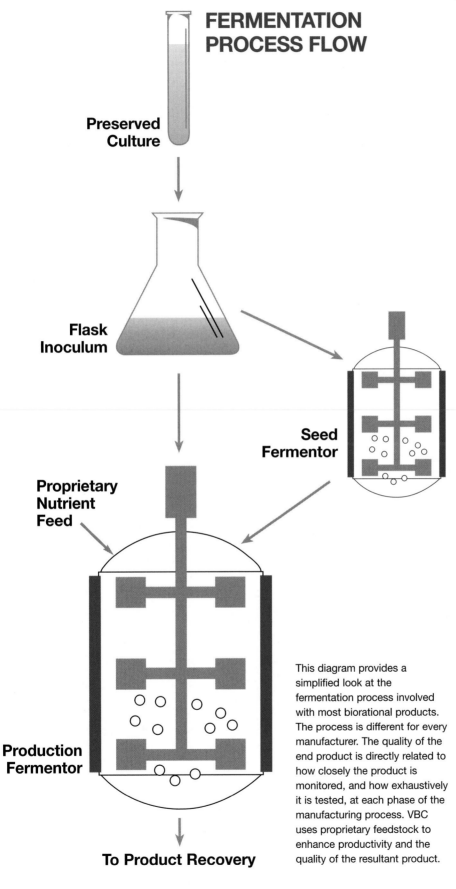

Preserved Culture

Flask Inoculum

Seed Fermentor

Proprietary Nutrient Feed

Production Fermentor

To Product Recovery

This diagram provides a simplified look at the fermentation process involved with most biorational products. The process is different for every manufacturer. The quality of the end product is directly related to how closely the product is monitored, and how exhaustively it is tested, at each phase of the manufacturing process. VBC uses proprietary feedstock to enhance productivity and the quality of the resultant product.

VALENT BIOSCIENCES. CORPORATION

Fermentation:
Not all Strains are
the Same

The bacterial strain itself is yet another variable that differs from supplier to supplier. Each manufacturer must obtain or maintain its own strains of inoculum, or baterial/fungal sources, to start product batches. These are living organisms, and so they are not identical. Product users need assurance that the bacterial strain the manufacturer uses will grow and reproduce robustly. Also, that it will produce the proper proportions and concentrations of proteins, so the final formulated product is not too weak or has the wrong profile for the job at hand.

Manufacturers do not sell microbial insecticides by default; those sales must be earned, grower by grower and season by season. To that end, VBC uses whatever resources necessary to make certain that its processes are consistent and able to produce high-quality, reliable products — every time.

Understanding Biorational Products

Fermentation:
Quality In, Quality Out

There is a maxim in operations management: It's far easier to build in quality from the beginning of the manufacturing process than insert it later. In other words, it's more efficient and less expensive to make it right the first time than to fix it if the process goes wrong.

In addition to using only the highest quality bacterial strains, the best manufacturing process hinges on using high quality raw materials for the growth medium. Ensuring only the highest quality materials are used is a critical part of quality control.

Since quality control begins with the very first input, VBC continuously and thoroughly evaluates suppliers for quality and reliability. All its vendors are required to certify that their products meet strict quality specifications. For example, VBC is a large consumer of field corn, which serves as a basic ingredient for fermentation. VBC conducts its own tests to verify vendor results, and if they don't meet specifications will immediately return the shipment. Each lot of raw materials accepted for use in the manufacturing process is traceable. Manufacturers are required to keep records so that each batch of final formulated product can be matched to an identifiable batch of materials. By managing this and other critical control points, VBC assures that optimum quality in the production environment bring optimum quality in the final product.

VALENT BioSciences. CORPORATION

Fermentation: Monitoring the Process

Another operations maxim is, "If you can't measure it, you can't manage it." VBC actively performs more than 100 measurements of 15 to 20 key process parameters during the fermentation process — every few minutes by computer-controlled sensors, and every eight hours by a human operator.

If, during the manufacturing process, parameters get outside the ideal ranges for development of the organism, the organism may become stressed and compromise the result. Only through constant testing and monitoring can VBC ensure these ranges are not breached. In addition to temperature and pH, tests include air flow (Bt is aerobic and needs plenty of environmental oxygen for efficient fermentation), back pressure in the reactor vessel, agitation (to provide proper aeration to the culture), and other proprietary traits.

Unless these optimum conditions are maintained, these organisms will not undergo vegetative reproduction as rapidly as is necessary. This results in reduced quantities of active material in the final product.

Cleanliness Means Consistency

Cleanliness is critical in fermentation manufacturing. Contaminants can lessen the efficacy or even destroy a production run, by retarding the development or otherwise harming the microorganisms that do the actual work.

For example, the bacterium used to make Bt insecticidal products are susceptible to infection by organisms known as bacteriophages (viruses that attack bacteria). Infection by bacteriophage can compromise the potency of the final product by weakening or killing the Bt, and the problem may not be discovered until the post-production assay. Avoiding contamination takes strict attention to cleanliness in the production facility and equipment at every step of the process, from the shake flask to the fermentation tank. VBC often uses redundant methods to preserve sterility; for example, air used for oxygenating fermentation vessels is heat-sterilized and then sterile filtered.

VALENT BIOSCIENCES. CORPORATION

Bioassays — A Key to Quality

One of the keys to the quality and consistency of VBC's microbial products is the emphasis on product testing throughout the manufacturing process. One such group of procedures involves specialized laboratory tests on insects or nematodes to measure the pesticidal activity of products as they are manufactured. These are called "bioassays."

VBC's vast experience with microbial products has yielded very specific data on how products should perform after each stage of production. As product makes its way from the smallest shake flask to the largest industrial fermentation tank, it is tested on target pests in the lab along the way — each time with very clear expectations.

To be effective, bioassays require a high degree of expertise and precision. For example, target insects, which serve as a control in each experiment, must be the same age, size, and state of health from test to test to test. Since expectations are based on how control insects respond, deviations between insect populations from one assay to the next would bring inconclusive results. These systems are also utilized in an R&D context to develop improved formulations and to screen for new strains.

Purity and Potency

A critical factor in successfully manufacturing both microbial and PGR products is final product purity. Unwanted contaminants in a final product can have a devastating effect on a crop. VBC employs proprietary processes both in the fermentation and recovery stages to ensure that its products meet stringent purity standards.

Unlike purity, potency for microbial products is a defined value of how much of a product is required to kill the target insect, a value that can vary between manufacturers. Several factors arising during the production process can affect the potency of the final formulated product. A temperature range outside the optimum for the microorganisms doing the work, the wrong nutrient balance in the fermentation tank, too much or too little agitation—all these can lead to a final product that contains of the proper active ingredient, but at less than the desired potency.

Fermentated products require a defined level of potency if they are to control pests effectively or conduct PGR activities, and to achieve the desired benefit in crop yield and/or quality. Enhanced yield and quality mean increased revenue to the grower, who incorporates such products into his program.

What the grower needs is assurance that the microbial pesticides or PGR products he or she uses meet the proper standard of potency every time. To protect its customers, Valent BioSciences tests both the active ingredient and formulated product for potency, thus assuring the product will perform with the intended result when properly used. In many cases, VBC also tests the product for potency against several target pest species, not just one. Many manufacturers list a potency rating for their microbial insecticides, but it is important to remember that potency values are both pest and manufacturer specific. With VBC's products, growers have the assurance that their products will perform as expected against a variety of labeled pests.

VALENT BioSciences.
CORPORATION

Ask About Your Supplier's Process

VBC is unique in that it produces its products to meet pharmaceutical grade standards. These standards are significantly more strict than what most manufacturers employ, and are the driving force behind the quality and consistency of the company's products. Here's a short list of key points you can focus on when discussing product attributes with a potential supplier:

☐ Product history

☐ Selected strains

☐ Raw materials

☐ How products are tested

☐ Quality assurance

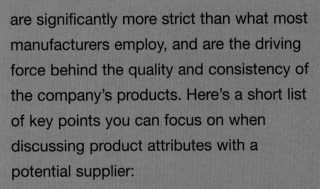

Other Success Factors: Formulation

Making Bt insecticides and PGRs more effective and easier to use is an ongoing process for the manufacturer.

A consistently high-quality technical active ingredient is only part of a winning crop production product. The other key element, at least in physical terms, is product formulation.

Valent BioSciences Corporation understands that formulation technology can be a product strength, particularly for microbial insecticides and plant growth regulators. VBC strives constantly to refine and enhance its formulated products to make them more efficacious and easier to use for growers around the world, many of whom have very specific needs with regard to crop or application method.

VALENT BIOSCIENCES
CORPORATION

PGR Formulation Technology

Plant growth regulators have very specific formulation requirements. As typically systemic products, they require good deposition on the plant surfaces, and then ready uptake. They do their work during critical and delicate stages of the crop's developmental cycle, and growers cannot afford the risk that formulation inerts will interact and have a negative effect on fruit finish.

Some growers produce to organic standards such as those published by the Organic Materials Review Institute (OMRI) in the United States, or to global Integrated Fruit Production (IFP) standards originally set forth by the European Union. These growers need effective PGRs to produce high-quality crops, yet must emply them in a system that conforms to defined standards.

At the same time, a company supplying PGRs prospers most when it is able to serve the needs of all growers of a particular crop with a single formulation of a given PGR, whether or not that grower produces to a restrictive or broad standard. In other words, the same formulation ought to meet the needs of "conventional," IPM, IFP, and organic growers alike with no sacrifice in efficacy, ease of use, or adherence to standards.

VBC has focused on meeting PGR needs of horticultural crop growers across the spectrum. It emphasizes the development of dust-free, instantly soluble formulations that do not incorporate organic solvents. This makes the products easier for growers to use, enhances crop safety, and makes most VBC products suitable for use in IPM, IFP and organic programs as well as in conventional production systems.

Formulated to Meet Market Needs

ProGibb 40% is an example of pioneering more highly concentrated formulations for PGRs that meet the needs of growers. The most concentrated gibberellic acid product on the market, this patented formulation is easy to use and extremely efficient. It is not dusty like a soluble powder and not as bulky as a liquid formulation.

Bt Insecticide Formulation Technology

In the Bt insecticide realm, VBC formulation research and development focuses on bringing to market formulations with a variety of characteristics desirable and beneficial for growers, crop advisors, retailers, and distributors.

One characteristic particularly useful in the global market is enhanced long-term stability and potency. VBC-formulated Bt products exhibit superior stability and can retain full potency in storage for years, even in tropical climates and in storage facilities lacking controlled conditions.

A dry flowable formulation of DiPel offers this degree of stability (Bt products are inherently more stable in non-aqueous, or non-water-based, systems). Other advantages of a dry-flowable formulation include: 1) a product that isn't dusty; 2) a product that is easier to handle; 3) a product that promotes better efficacy; 4) a product that mixes more quickly.

Also important are formulations incorporating protectants that help Bt insecticides withstand the solar spectrum longer in field conditions. VBC features dry-spray technology, which helps encapsulate the protein crystals, with enhancements during formulation that allow extended product performance even after exposure to sunlight.

Formula for Success

The most successful companies conduct extensive field testing of new formulations in order to ensure the highest degree of efficacy and crop safety, before bringing products to market. When selecting a biorationals partner, make sure you choose one with a proven history of performance in this area.

Formulated to Meet Market Needs

VBC provides dry flowable formulations for Bt insecticides such as DiPel and XenTari. A high potency technical active ingredient coupled with highly concentrated formulations allows low spray volumes, ideal for many growers. The company recommends use of a spreader-sticker to aid deposition and rainfastness, particularly for agronomic crops such as cotton.

VALENT BIOSCIENCES CORPORATION

A Look at Product and Market Development

Products developed with a customer-focus work best in a grower's program.

Product Development

Simply stated, the end user should always be the starting point of product development. In developing its product line, Valent BioSciences Corporation begins with unmet customer needs and works toward a final product that fits with the company's core competencies. This "what the market needs" approach gives its customers an advantage, and allows VBC to operate within the areas it is best positioned to succeed.

The PGR and biological insecticide segments are unlike "conventional" crop protection in that there is not a constant flow of new active ingredients coming down the product-development pipeline. With biorationals, unique benefits can be obtained through subtle variations in strains or formulations, and this focus is the cornerstone of VBC's product development strategy.

Market Development

New crop varieties enter markets constantly. Application technology changes. Growers need to take advantage of exciting new commercial possibilities these changes represent. Working with growers and experienced agronomists and horticulturalists, VBC conducts continuous research to help develop and refine products and formulations for enhanced field performance.

New products are not the only way to meet market needs. Bringing or adapting existing products into new markets is another. While most of the top agricultural crop producers already use products such as Bt insecticides and PGRs, not all are aware of their benefits. VBC often takes the role of "pioneer," helping growers and other agricultural professionals become more aware of the value and return on investment these products provide.

A Look at Product Support

High-quality crop protection products are a necessity for any grower, particularly in high-value specialty horticultural crop markets. But growers and distributors also depend on a strong support system for critical product information.

When selecting a biorational product supplier, accessibility and experience counts. With more than 40 years as a biorationals manufacturer, VBC sees itself as a powerful ally that combines product knowledge with formulation technology, efficacy, and product reliability. Anywhere in the world, a grower, crop advisor, retailer, or distributor can reach a sales or technical representative of VBC or its parent company, Sumitomo Chemical, who can answer questions about product application, timing, and a host of other issues that can ensure a high quality crop.

Remember: Treatment windows for PGRs on some crops can be as narrow as a day or two. While the potential for significant fruit quality increase is high, growers don't want to make an application timing error that could compromise the effects of these products. Most growers have plenty of experience using ProGibb, for example, to raise more valuable crops. But having access to the expertise of VBC personnel helps growers and crop advisors manage risk.

VALENT BioSciences.
CORPORATION

Focus and Commitment

Valent BioSciences Corporation would like to take this opportunity to thank you for your interest in learning more about biorational products. As a company with more than 40 years experience in the development, manufacture, sale, and support of biorationals, VBC is completely focused and wholly invested on the growth and sustainability of this category.

Known throughout the world as the best in its class for biorational product formulation, quality control, and the level of service provided to its customers, VBC is committed to knowledge transfer regarding the benefits of these valuable tools. This guide may not answer every question you have about biorationals, but we hope that the information we've presented here will stimulate new thoughts and possibilities for both current and future users of these products.

We welcome both your comments and inquiries about how we can help you grow your business.

Valent BioSciences Corporation